FRIDAY

Distance: _____

Time: _____

Speed: _____

Weather: _____

Calories burned: _____

SATURDAY

Distance: _____

Time: _____

Speed: _____

Weather: _____

Calories burned: _____

Notes:

SUNDAY

Distance: _____

Time: _____

Speed: _____

Weather: _____

Calories burned: _____

Notes:

WEEKLY REVIEW

Total distance: _____

Total hours: _____

Average speed: _____

Total calories burned: _____

Weight: _____

Notes:

Week starting:_____

MONDAY

Distance:_____

Time:_____

Speed:_____

Weather:_____

Calories burned:_____

Notes:

TUESDAY

Distance:_____

Time:_____

Speed:_____

Weather:_____

Calories burned:_____

Notes:

WEDNESDAY

Distance:_____

Time:_____

Speed:_____

Weather:_____

Calories burned:_____

Notes:

THURSDAY

Distance:_____

Time:_____

Speed:_____

Weather:_____

Calories burned:_____

Notes:

FRIDAY

Distance: _____

Time: _____

Speed: _____

Weather: _____

Calories burned: _____

Notes:

SATURDAY

Distance: _____

Time: _____

Speed: _____

Weather: _____

Calories burned: _____

Notes:

SUNDAY

Distance: _____

Time: _____

Speed: _____

Weather: _____

Calories burned: _____

Notes:

WEEKLY REVIEW

Total distance: _____

Total hours: _____

Average speed: _____

Total calories burned: _____

Weight: _____

Notes:

Week starting:_____

MONDAY

Distance: _____

Time: _____

Speed: _____

Weather: _____

Calories burned: _____

Notes:

TUESDAY

Distance: _____

Time: _____

Speed: _____

Weather: _____

Calories burned: _____

Notes:

WEDNESDAY

Distance: _____

Time: _____

Speed: _____

Weather: _____

Calories burned: _____

Notes:

THURSDAY

Distance: _____

Time: _____

Speed: _____

Weather: _____

Calories burned: _____

Notes:

FRIDAY

Distance:

Time:

Speed:

Weather:

Calories burned:

Notes:

SATURDAY

Distance:

Time:

Speed:

Weather:

Calories burned:

Notes:

SUNDAY

Distance:

Time:

Speed:

Weather:

Calories burned:

Notes:

WEEKLY REVIEW

Total distance:

Total hours:

Average speed:

Total calories burned:

Weight:

Notes:

Week starting:_____

MONDAY

Distance: _____

Time: _____

Speed: _____

Weather: _____

Calories burned: _____

Notes:

TUESDAY

Distance: _____

Time: _____

Speed: _____

Weather: _____

Calories burned: _____

Notes:

WEDNESDAY

Distance: _____

Time: _____

Speed: _____

Weather: _____

Calories burned: _____

Notes:

THURSDAY

Distance: _____

Time: _____

Speed: _____

Weather: _____

Calories burned: _____

Notes:

FRIDAY

Distance: _____

Time: _____

Speed: _____

Weather: _____

Calories burned: _____

Notes:

SATURDAY

Distance: _____

Time: _____

Speed: _____

Weather: _____

Calories burned: _____

Notes:

SUNDAY

Distance: _____

Time: _____

Speed: _____

Weather: _____

Calories burned: _____

Notes:

WEEKLY REVIEW

Total distance: _____

Total hours: _____

Average speed: _____

Total calories burned: _____

Weight: _____

Notes:

Week starting:_____

MONDAY

Distance: _____

Time: _____

Speed: _____

Weather: _____

Calories burned: _____

Notes:

TUESDAY

Distance: _____

Time: _____

Speed: _____

Weather: _____

Calories burned: _____

Notes:

WEDNESDAY

Distance: _____

Time: _____

Speed: _____

Weather: _____

Calories burned: _____

Notes:

THURSDAY

Distance: _____

Time: _____

Speed: _____

Weather: _____

Calories burned: _____

Notes:

FRIDAY

Distance: _____

Time: _____

Speed: _____

Weather: _____

Calories burned: _____

Notes:

SATURDAY

Distance: _____

Time: _____

Speed: _____

Weather: _____

Calories burned: _____

Notes:

SUNDAY

Distance: _____

Time: _____

Speed: _____

Weather: _____

Calories burned: _____

Notes:

WEEKLY REVIEW

Total distance: _____

Total hours: _____

Average speed: _____

Total calories burned: _____

Weight: _____

Notes:

Week starting:_____

MONDAY

Distance:_____

Time:_____

Speed:_____

Weather:_____

Calories burned:_____

Notes:

TUESDAY

Distance:_____

Time:_____

Speed:_____

Weather:_____

Calories burned:_____

Notes:

WEDNESDAY

Distance:_____

Time:_____

Speed:_____

Weather:_____

Calories burned:_____

Notes:

THURSDAY

Distance:_____

Time:_____

Speed:_____

Weather:_____

Calories burned:_____

Notes:

FRIDAY

Distance: _____

Time: _____

Speed: _____

Weather: _____

Calories burned: _____

Notes:

SATURDAY

Distance: _____

Time: _____

Speed: _____

Weather: _____

Calories burned: _____

Notes:

SUNDAY

Distance: _____

Time: _____

Speed: _____

Weather: _____

Calories burned: _____

Notes:

WEEKLY REVIEW

Total distance: _____

Total hours: _____

Average speed: _____

Total calories burned: _____

Weight: _____

Notes:

Week starting:_____

MONDAY

Distance:_____

Time:_____

Speed:_____

Weather:_____

Calories burned:_____

Notes:

TUESDAY

Distance:_____

Time:_____

Speed:_____

Weather:_____

Calories burned:_____

Notes:

WEDNESDAY

Distance:_____

Time:_____

Speed:_____

Weather:_____

Calories burned:_____

Notes:

THURSDAY

Distance:_____

Time:_____

Speed:_____

Weather:_____

Calories burned:_____

Notes:

FRIDAY

Distance: _____

Time: _____

Speed: _____

Weather: _____

Calories burned: _____

Notes:

SATURDAY

Distance: _____

Time: _____

Speed: _____

Weather: _____

Calories burned: _____

Notes:

SUNDAY

Distance: _____

Time: _____

Speed: _____

Weather: _____

Calories burned: _____

Notes:

WEEKLY REVIEW

Total distance: _____

Total hours: _____

Average speed: _____

Total calories burned: _____

Weight: _____

Notes:

Week starting:_____

MONDAY

Distance:_____

Time:_____

Speed:_____

Weather:_____

Calories burned:_____

Notes:

TUESDAY

Distance:_____

Time:_____

Speed:_____

Weather:_____

Calories burned:_____

Notes:

WEDNESDAY

Distance:_____

Time:_____

Speed:_____

Weather:_____

Calories burned:_____

Notes:

THURSDAY

Distance:_____

Time:_____

Speed:_____

Weather:_____

Calories burned:_____

Notes:

FRIDAY

Distance: _____

Time: _____

Speed: _____

Weather: _____

Calories burned: _____

Notes:

SATURDAY

Distance: _____

Time: _____

Speed: _____

Weather: _____

Calories burned: _____

Notes:

SUNDAY

Distance: _____

Time: _____

Speed: _____

Weather: _____

Calories burned: _____

Notes:

WEEKLY REVIEW

Total distance: _____

Total hours: _____

Average speed: _____

Total calories burned: _____

Weight: _____

Notes:

Week starting:_____

MONDAY

Distance: _____

Time: _____

Speed: _____

Weather: _____

Calories burned: _____

Notes:

TUESDAY

Distance: _____

Time: _____

Speed: _____

Weather: _____

Calories burned: _____

Notes:

WEDNESDAY

Distance: _____

Time: _____

Speed: _____

Weather: _____

Calories burned: _____

Notes:

THURSDAY

Distance: _____

Time: _____

Speed: _____

Weather: _____

Calories burned: _____

Notes:

FRIDAY

Distance:

Time:

Speed:

Weather:

Calories burned:

Notes:

SATURDAY

Distance:

Time:

Speed:

Weather:

Calories burned:

Notes:

SUNDAY

Distance:

Time:

Speed:

Weather:

Calories burned:

Notes:

WEEKLY REVIEW

Total distance:

Total hours:

Average speed:

Total calories burned:

Weight:

Notes:

Week starting:_____

MONDAY

Distance:_____

Time:_____

Speed:_____

Weather:_____

Calories burned:_____

Notes:

TUESDAY

Distance:_____

Time:_____

Speed:_____

Weather:_____

Calories burned:_____

Notes:

WEDNESDAY

Distance:_____

Time:_____

Speed:_____

Weather:_____

Calories burned:_____

Notes:

THURSDAY

Distance:_____

Time:_____

Speed:_____

Weather:_____

Calories burned:_____

Notes:

FRIDAY

Distance: _____

Time: _____

Speed: _____

Weather: _____

Calories burned: _____

Notes:

SATURDAY

Distance: _____

Time: _____

Speed: _____

Weather: _____

Calories burned: _____

Notes:

SUNDAY

Distance: _____

Time: _____

Speed: _____

Weather: _____

Calories burned: _____

Notes:

WEEKLY REVIEW

Total distance: _____

Total hours: _____

Average speed: _____

Total calories burned: _____

Weight: _____

Notes:

Week starting:_____

MONDAY

Distance:_____

Time:_____

Speed:_____

Weather:_____

Calories burned:_____

Notes:

TUESDAY

Distance:_____

Time:_____

Speed:_____

Weather:_____

Calories burned:_____

Notes:

WEDNESDAY

Distance:_____

Time:_____

Speed:_____

Weather:_____

Calories burned:_____

Notes:

THURSDAY

Distance:_____

Time:_____

Speed:_____

Weather:_____

Calories burned:_____

Notes:

FRIDAY

Distance: _____

Time: _____

Speed: _____

Weather: _____

Calories burned: _____

Notes:

SATURDAY

Distance: _____

Time: _____

Speed: _____

Weather: _____

Calories burned: _____

Notes:

SUNDAY

Distance: _____

Time: _____

Speed: _____

Weather: _____

Calories burned: _____

Notes:

WEEKLY REVIEW

Total distance: _____

Total hours: _____

Average speed: _____

Total calories burned: _____

Weight: _____

Notes:

Week starting:_____

MONDAY

Distance: _____

Time: _____

Speed: _____

Weather: _____

Calories burned: _____

Notes:

TUESDAY

Distance: _____

Time: _____

Speed: _____

Weather: _____

Calories burned: _____

Notes:

WEDNESDAY

Distance: _____

Time: _____

Speed: _____

Weather: _____

Calories burned: _____

Notes:

THURSDAY

Distance: _____

Time: _____

Speed: _____

Weather: _____

Calories burned: _____

Notes:

FRIDAY

Distance: _____

Time: _____

Speed: _____

Weather: _____

Calories burned: _____

Notes:

SATURDAY

Distance: _____

Time: _____

Speed: _____

Weather: _____

Calories burned: _____

Notes:

SUNDAY

Distance: _____

Time: _____

Speed: _____

Weather: _____

Calories burned: _____

Notes:

WEEKLY REVIEW

Total distance: _____

Total hours: _____

Average speed: _____

Total calories burned: _____

Weight: _____

Notes:

Week starting:_____

MONDAY

Distance:_____

Time:_____

Speed:_____

Weather:_____

Calories burned:_____

Notes:

TUESDAY

Distance:_____

Time:_____

Speed:_____

Weather:_____

Calories burned:_____

Notes:

WEDNESDAY

Distance:_____

Time:_____

Speed:_____

Weather:_____

Calories burned:_____

Notes:

THURSDAY

Distance:_____

Time:_____

Speed:_____

Weather:_____

Calories burned:_____

Notes:

FRIDAY

Distance: _____

Time: _____

Speed: _____

Weather: _____

Calories burned: _____

Notes:

SATURDAY

Distance: _____

Time: _____

Speed: _____

Weather: _____

Calories burned: _____

Notes:

SUNDAY

Distance: _____

Time: _____

Speed: _____

Weather: _____

Calories burned: _____

Notes:

WEEKLY REVIEW

Total distance: _____

Total hours: _____

Average speed: _____

Total calories burned: _____

Weight: _____

Notes:

Week starting:_____

MONDAY

Distance: _____

Time: _____

Speed: _____

Weather: _____

Calories burned: _____

Notes:

TUESDAY

Distance: _____

Time: _____

Speed: _____

Weather: _____

Calories burned: _____

Notes:

WEDNESDAY

Distance: _____

Time: _____

Speed: _____

Weather: _____

Calories burned: _____

Notes:

THURSDAY

Distance: _____

Time: _____

Speed: _____

Weather: _____

Calories burned: _____

Notes:

FRIDAY

Distance: _____

Time: _____

Speed: _____

Weather: _____

Calories burned: _____

Notes:

SATURDAY

Distance: _____

Time: _____

Speed: _____

Weather: _____

Calories burned: _____

Notes:

SUNDAY

Distance: _____

Time: _____

Speed: _____

Weather: _____

Calories burned: _____

Notes:

WEEKLY REVIEW

Total distance: _____

Total hours: _____

Average speed: _____

Total calories burned: _____

Weight: _____

Notes:

Week starting:_____

MONDAY

Distance:_____

Time:_____

Speed:_____

Weather:_____

Calories burned:_____

Notes:

TUESDAY

Distance:_____

Time:_____

Speed:_____

Weather:_____

Calories burned:_____

Notes:

WEDNESDAY

Distance:_____

Time:_____

Speed:_____

Weather:_____

Calories burned:_____

Notes:

THURSDAY

Distance:_____

Time:_____

Speed:_____

Weather:_____

Calories burned:_____

Notes:

FRIDAY

Distance: _____

Time: _____

Speed: _____

Weather: _____

Calories burned: _____

Notes:

SATURDAY

Distance: _____

Time: _____

Speed: _____

Weather: _____

Calories burned: _____

Notes:

SUNDAY

Distance: _____

Time: _____

Speed: _____

Weather: _____

Calories burned: _____

Notes:

WEEKLY REVIEW

Total distance: _____

Total hours: _____

Average speed: _____

Total calories burned: _____

Weight: _____

Notes:

Week starting:_____

MONDAY

Distance: _____

Time: _____

Speed: _____

Weather: _____

Calories burned: _____

Notes:

TUESDAY

Distance: _____

Time: _____

Speed: _____

Weather: _____

Calories burned: _____

Notes:

WEDNESDAY

Distance: _____

Time: _____

Speed: _____

Weather: _____

Calories burned: _____

Notes:

THURSDAY

Distance: _____

Time: _____

Speed: _____

Weather: _____

Calories burned: _____

Notes:

FRIDAY

Distance: _____

Time: _____

Speed: _____

Weather: _____

Calories burned: _____

Notes:

SATURDAY

Distance: _____

Time: _____

Speed: _____

Weather: _____

Calories burned: _____

Notes:

SUNDAY

Distance: _____

Time: _____

Speed: _____

Weather: _____

Calories burned: _____

Notes:

WEEKLY REVIEW

Total distance: _____

Total hours: _____

Average speed: _____

Total calories burned: _____

Weight: _____

Notes:

Week starting:_____

MONDAY

Distance:_____

Time:_____

Speed:_____

Weather:_____

Calories burned:_____

Notes:

TUESDAY

Distance:_____

Time:_____

Speed:_____

Weather:_____

Calories burned:_____

Notes:

WEDNESDAY

Distance:_____

Time:_____

Speed:_____

Weather:_____

Calories burned:_____

Notes:

THURSDAY

Distance:_____

Time:_____

Speed:_____

Weather:_____

Calories burned:_____

Notes:

FRIDAY

Distance: _____

Time: _____

Speed: _____

Weather: _____

Calories burned: _____

Notes:

SATURDAY

Distance: _____

Time: _____

Speed: _____

Weather: _____

Calories burned: _____

Notes:

SUNDAY

Distance: _____

Time: _____

Speed: _____

Weather: _____

Calories burned: _____

Notes:

WEEKLY REVIEW

Total distance: _____

Total hours: _____

Average speed: _____

Total calories burned: _____

Weight: _____

Notes:

Week starting:_____

MONDAY

Distance: _____

Time: _____

Speed: _____

Weather: _____

Calories burned: _____

Notes:

TUESDAY

Distance: _____

Time: _____

Speed: _____

Weather: _____

Calories burned: _____

Notes:

WEDNESDAY

Distance: _____

Time: _____

Speed: _____

Weather: _____

Calories burned: _____

Notes:

THURSDAY

Distance: _____

Time: _____

Speed: _____

Weather: _____

Calories burned: _____

Notes:

FRIDAY

Distance: _____

Time: _____

Speed: _____

Weather: _____

Calories burned: _____

Notes:

SATURDAY

Distance: _____

Time: _____

Speed: _____

Weather: _____

Calories burned: _____

Notes:

SUNDAY

Distance: _____

Time: _____

Speed: _____

Weather: _____

Calories burned: _____

Notes:

WEEKLY REVIEW

Total distance: _____

Total hours: _____

Average speed: _____

Total calories burned: _____

Weight: _____

Notes:

Week starting:_____

MONDAY

Distance:_____

Time:_____

Speed:_____

Weather:_____

Calories burned:_____

Notes:

TUESDAY

Distance:_____

Time:_____

Speed:_____

Weather:_____

Calories burned:_____

Notes:

WEDNESDAY

Distance:_____

Time:_____

Speed:_____

Weather:_____

Calories burned:_____

Notes:

THURSDAY

Distance:_____

Time:_____

Speed:_____

Weather:_____

Calories burned:_____

Notes:

FRIDAY

Distance: _____

Time: _____

Speed: _____

Weather: _____

Calories burned: _____

Notes:

SATURDAY

Distance: _____

Time: _____

Speed: _____

Weather: _____

Calories burned: _____

Notes:

SUNDAY

Distance: _____

Time: _____

Speed: _____

Weather: _____

Calories burned: _____

Notes:

WEEKLY REVIEW

Total distance: _____

Total hours: _____

Average speed: _____

Total calories burned: _____

Weight: _____

Notes:

Week starting:_____

MONDAY

Distance:_____

Time:_____

Speed:_____

Weather:_____

Calories burned:_____

Notes:

TUESDAY

Distance:_____

Time:_____

Speed:_____

Weather:_____

Calories burned:_____

Notes:

WEDNESDAY

Distance:_____

Time:_____

Speed:_____

Weather:_____

Calories burned:_____

Notes:

THURSDAY

Distance:_____

Time:_____

Speed:_____

Weather:_____

Calories burned:_____

Notes:

FRIDAY

Distance: _____

Time: _____

Speed: _____

Weather: _____

Calories burned: _____

Notes:

SATURDAY

Distance: _____

Time: _____

Speed: _____

Weather: _____

Calories burned: _____

Notes:

SUNDAY

Distance: _____

Time: _____

Speed: _____

Weather: _____

Calories burned: _____

Notes:

WEEKLY REVIEW

Total distance: _____

Total hours: _____

Average speed: _____

Total calories burned: _____

Weight: _____

Notes:

Week starting:_____

MONDAY

Distance: _____

Time: _____

Speed: _____

Weather: _____

Calories burned: _____

Notes:

TUESDAY

Distance: _____

Time: _____

Speed: _____

Weather: _____

Calories burned: _____

Notes:

WEDNESDAY

Distance: _____

Time: _____

Speed: _____

Weather: _____

Calories burned: _____

Notes:

THURSDAY

Distance: _____

Time: _____

Speed: _____

Weather: _____

Calories burned: _____

Notes:

FRIDAY

Distance: _____

Time: _____

Speed: _____

Weather: _____

Calories burned: _____

Notes:

SATURDAY

Distance: _____

Time: _____

Speed: _____

Weather: _____

Calories burned: _____

Notes:

SUNDAY

Distance: _____

Time: _____

Speed: _____

Weather: _____

Calories burned: _____

Notes:

WEEKLY REVIEW

Total distance: _____

Total hours: _____

Average speed: _____

Total calories burned: _____

Weight: _____

Notes:

Week starting:_____

MONDAY

Distance: _____

Time: _____

Speed: _____

Weather: _____

Calories burned: _____

Notes:

TUESDAY

Distance: _____

Time: _____

Speed: _____

Weather: _____

Calories burned: _____

Notes:

WEDNESDAY

Distance: _____

Time: _____

Speed: _____

Weather: _____

Calories burned: _____

Notes:

THURSDAY

Distance: _____

Time: _____

Speed: _____

Weather: _____

Calories burned: _____

Notes:

FRIDAY

Distance: _____

Time: _____

Speed: _____

Weather: _____

Calories burned: _____

Notes:

SATURDAY

Distance: _____

Time: _____

Speed: _____

Weather: _____

Calories burned: _____

Notes:

SUNDAY

Distance: _____

Time: _____

Speed: _____

Weather: _____

Calories burned: _____

Notes:

WEEKLY REVIEW

Total distance: _____

Total hours: _____

Average speed: _____

Total calories burned: _____

Weight: _____

Notes:

Week starting:_____

MONDAY

Distance: _____

Time: _____

Speed: _____

Weather: _____

Calories burned: _____

Notes:

TUESDAY

Distance: _____

Time: _____

Speed: _____

Weather: _____

Calories burned: _____

Notes:

WEDNESDAY

Distance: _____

Time: _____

Speed: _____

Weather: _____

Calories burned: _____

Notes:

THURSDAY

Distance: _____

Time: _____

Speed: _____

Weather: _____

Calories burned: _____

Notes:

FRIDAY

Distance: _____

Time: _____

Speed: _____

Weather: _____

Calories burned: _____

Notes:

SATURDAY

Distance: _____

Time: _____

Speed: _____

Weather: _____

Calories burned: _____

Notes:

SUNDAY

Distance: _____

Time: _____

Speed: _____

Weather: _____

Calories burned: _____

Notes:

WEEKLY REVIEW

Total distance: _____

Total hours: _____

Average speed: _____

Total calories burned: _____

Weight: _____

Notes:

Week starting:_____

MONDAY

Distance: _____

Time: _____

Speed: _____

Weather: _____

Calories burned: _____

Notes:

TUESDAY

Distance: _____

Time: _____

Speed: _____

Weather: _____

Calories burned: _____

Notes:

WEDNESDAY

Distance: _____

Time: _____

Speed: _____

Weather: _____

Calories burned: _____

Notes:

THURSDAY

Distance: _____

Time: _____

Speed: _____

Weather: _____

Calories burned: _____

Notes:

FRIDAY

Distance:

Time:

Speed:

Weather:

Calories burned:

Notes:

SATURDAY

Distance:

Time:

Speed:

Weather:

Calories burned:

Notes:

SUNDAY

Distance:

Time:

Speed:

Weather:

Calories burned:

Notes:

WEEKLY REVIEW

Total distance:

Total hours:

Average speed:

Total calories burned:

Weight:

Notes:

Week starting:_____

MONDAY

Distance:_____

Time:_____

Speed:_____

Weather:_____

Calories burned:_____

Notes:

TUESDAY

Distance:_____

Time:_____

Speed:_____

Weather:_____

Calories burned:_____

Notes:

WEDNESDAY

Distance:_____

Time:_____

Speed:_____

Weather:_____

Calories burned:_____

Notes:

THURSDAY

Distance:_____

Time:_____

Speed:_____

Weather:_____

Calories burned:_____

Notes:

FRIDAY

Distance: _____

Time: _____

Speed: _____

Weather: _____

Calories burned: _____

Notes:

SATURDAY

Distance: _____

Time: _____

Speed: _____

Weather: _____

Calories burned: _____

Notes:

SUNDAY

Distance: _____

Time: _____

Speed: _____

Weather: _____

Calories burned: _____

Notes:

WEEKLY REVIEW

Total distance: _____

Total hours: _____

Average speed: _____

Total calories burned: _____

Weight: _____

Notes:

Week starting:_____

MONDAY

Distance:_____

Time:_____

Speed:_____

Weather:_____

Calories burned:_____

Notes:

TUESDAY

Distance:_____

Time:_____

Speed:_____

Weather:_____

Calories burned:_____

Notes:

WEDNESDAY

Distance:_____

Time:_____

Speed:_____

Weather:_____

Calories burned:_____

Notes:

THURSDAY

Distance:_____

Time:_____

Speed:_____

Weather:_____

Calories burned:_____

Notes:

FRIDAY

Distance: _____

Time: _____

Speed: _____

Weather: _____

Calories burned: _____

Notes:

SATURDAY

Distance: _____

Time: _____

Speed: _____

Weather: _____

Calories burned: _____

Notes:

SUNDAY

Distance: _____

Time: _____

Speed: _____

Weather: _____

Calories burned: _____

Notes:

WEEKLY REVIEW

Total distance: _____

Total hours: _____

Average speed: _____

Total calories burned: _____

Weight: _____

Notes:

Week starting:_____

MONDAY

Distance: _____

Time: _____

Speed: _____

Weather: _____

Calories burned: _____

Notes:

TUESDAY

Distance: _____

Time: _____

Speed: _____

Weather: _____

Calories burned: _____

Notes:

WEDNESDAY

Distance: _____

Time: _____

Speed: _____

Weather: _____

Calories burned: _____

Notes:

THURSDAY

Distance: _____

Time: _____

Speed: _____

Weather: _____

Calories burned: _____

Notes:

FRIDAY

Distance:

Time:

Speed:

Weather:

Calories burned:

Notes:

SATURDAY

Distance:

Time:

Speed:

Weather:

Calories burned:

Notes:

SUNDAY

Distance:

Time:

Speed:

Weather:

Calories burned:

Notes:

WEEKLY REVIEW

Total distance:

Total hours:

Average speed:

Total calories burned:

Weight:

Notes:

Week starting:_____

MONDAY

Distance:_____

Time:_____

Speed:_____

Weather:_____

Calories burned:_____

Notes:

TUESDAY

Distance:_____

Time:_____

Speed:_____

Weather:_____

Calories burned:_____

Notes:

WEDNESDAY

Distance:_____

Time:_____

Speed:_____

Weather:_____

Calories burned:_____

Notes:

THURSDAY

Distance:_____

Time:_____

Speed:_____

Weather:_____

Calories burned:_____

Notes:

FRIDAY

Distance: _____

Time: _____

Speed: _____

Weather: _____

Calories burned: _____

Notes:

SATURDAY

Distance: _____

Time: _____

Speed: _____

Weather: _____

Calories burned: _____

Notes:

SUNDAY

Distance: _____

Time: _____

Speed: _____

Weather: _____

Calories burned: _____

Notes:

WEEKLY REVIEW

Total distance: _____

Total hours: _____

Average speed: _____

Total calories burned: _____

Weight: _____

Notes:

Week starting: _____

MONDAY

Distance: _____

Time: _____

Speed: _____

Weather: _____

Calories burned: _____

Notes:

TUESDAY

Distance: _____

Time: _____

Speed: _____

Weather: _____

Calories burned: _____

Notes:

WEDNESDAY

Distance: _____

Time: _____

Speed: _____

Weather: _____

Calories burned: _____

Notes:

THURSDAY

Distance: _____

Time: _____

Speed: _____

Weather: _____

Calories burned: _____

Notes:

FRIDAY

Distance: _____

Time: _____

Speed: _____

Weather: _____

Calories burned: _____

Notes:

SATURDAY

Distance: _____

Time: _____

Speed: _____

Weather: _____

Calories burned: _____

Notes:

SUNDAY

Distance: _____

Time: _____

Speed: _____

Weather: _____

Calories burned: _____

Notes:

WEEKLY REVIEW

Total distance: _____

Total hours: _____

Average speed: _____

Total calories burned: _____

Weight: _____

Notes:

Week starting:_____

MONDAY

Distance: _____

Time: _____

Speed: _____

Weather: _____

Calories burned: _____

Notes:

TUESDAY

Distance: _____

Time: _____

Speed: _____

Weather: _____

Calories burned: _____

Notes:

WEDNESDAY

Distance: _____

Time: _____

Speed: _____

Weather: _____

Calories burned: _____

Notes:

THURSDAY

Distance: _____

Time: _____

Speed: _____

Weather: _____

Calories burned: _____

Notes:

FRIDAY

Distance: _____

Time: _____

Speed: _____

Weather: _____

Calories burned: _____

Notes:

SATURDAY

Distance: _____

Time: _____

Speed: _____

Weather: _____

Calories burned: _____

Notes:

SUNDAY

Distance: _____

Time: _____

Speed: _____

Weather: _____

Calories burned: _____

Notes:

WEEKLY REVIEW

Total distance: _____

Total hours: _____

Average speed: _____

Total calories burned: _____

Weight: _____

Notes:

Week starting:_____

MONDAY

Distance: _____

Time: _____

Speed: _____

Weather: _____

Calories burned: _____

Notes:

TUESDAY

Distance: _____

Time: _____

Speed: _____

Weather: _____

Calories burned: _____

Notes:

WEDNESDAY

Distance: _____

Time: _____

Speed: _____

Weather: _____

Calories burned: _____

Notes:

THURSDAY

Distance: _____

Time: _____

Speed: _____

Weather: _____

Calories burned: _____

Notes:

FRIDAY

Distance: _____

Time: _____

Speed: _____

Weather: _____

Calories burned: _____

Notes:

SATURDAY

Distance: _____

Time: _____

Speed: _____

Weather: _____

Calories burned: _____

Notes:

SUNDAY

Distance: _____

Time: _____

Speed: _____

Weather: _____

Calories burned: _____

Notes:

WEEKLY REVIEW

Total distance: _____

Total hours: _____

Average speed: _____

Total calories burned: _____

Weight: _____

Notes:

Week starting:_____

MONDAY

Distance:_____

Time:_____

Speed:_____

Weather:_____

Calories burned:_____

Notes:

TUESDAY

Distance:_____

Time:_____

Speed:_____

Weather:_____

Calories burned:_____

Notes:

WEDNESDAY

Distance:_____

Time:_____

Speed:_____

Weather:_____

Calories burned:_____

Notes:

THURSDAY

Distance:_____

Time:_____

Speed:_____

Weather:_____

Calories burned:_____

Notes:

FRIDAY

Distance: _____

Time: _____

Speed: _____

Weather: _____

Calories burned: _____

Notes:

SATURDAY

Distance: _____

Time: _____

Speed: _____

Weather: _____

Calories burned: _____

Notes:

SUNDAY

Distance: _____

Time: _____

Speed: _____

Weather: _____

Calories burned: _____

Notes:

WEEKLY REVIEW

Total distance: _____

Total hours: _____

Average speed: _____

Total calories burned: _____

Weight: _____

Notes:

Week starting:_____

MONDAY

Distance: _____

Time: _____

Speed: _____

Weather: _____

Calories burned: _____

Notes:

TUESDAY

Distance: _____

Time: _____

Speed: _____

Weather: _____

Calories burned: _____

Notes:

WEDNESDAY

Distance: _____

Time: _____

Speed: _____

Weather: _____

Calories burned: _____

Notes:

THURSDAY

Distance: _____

Time: _____

Speed: _____

Weather: _____

Calories burned: _____

Notes:

FRIDAY

Distance: _____

Time: _____

Speed: _____

Weather: _____

Calories burned: _____

Notes:

SATURDAY

Distance: _____

Time: _____

Speed: _____

Weather: _____

Calories burned: _____

Notes:

SUNDAY

Distance: _____

Time: _____

Speed: _____

Weather: _____

Calories burned: _____

Notes:

WEEKLY REVIEW

Total distance: _____

Total hours: _____

Average speed: _____

Total calories burned: _____

Weight: _____

Notes:

Week starting:_____

MONDAY

Distance: _____

Time: _____

Speed: _____

Weather: _____

Calories burned: _____

Notes:

TUESDAY

Distance: _____

Time: _____

Speed: _____

Weather: _____

Calories burned: _____

Notes:

WEDNESDAY

Distance: _____

Time: _____

Speed: _____

Weather: _____

Calories burned: _____

Notes:

THURSDAY

Distance: _____

Time: _____

Speed: _____

Weather: _____

Calories burned: _____

Notes:

FRIDAY

Distance: _____

Time: _____

Speed: _____

Weather: _____

Calories burned: _____

Notes:

SATURDAY

Distance: _____

Time: _____

Speed: _____

Weather: _____

Calories burned: _____

Notes:

SUNDAY

Distance: _____

Time: _____

Speed: _____

Weather: _____

Calories burned: _____

Notes:

WEEKLY REVIEW

Total distance: _____

Total hours: _____

Average speed: _____

Total calories burned: _____

Weight: _____

Notes:

Week starting:_____

MONDAY

Distance:_____

Time:_____

Speed:_____

Weather:_____

Calories burned:_____

Notes:

TUESDAY

Distance:_____

Time:_____

Speed:_____

Weather:_____

Calories burned:_____

Notes:

WEDNESDAY

Distance:_____

Time:_____

Speed:_____

Weather:_____

Calories burned:_____

Notes:

THURSDAY

Distance:_____

Time:_____

Speed:_____

Weather:_____

Calories burned:_____

Notes:

FRIDAY

Distance: _____

Time: _____

Speed: _____

Weather: _____

Calories burned: _____

Notes:

SATURDAY

Distance: _____

Time: _____

Speed: _____

Weather: _____

Calories burned: _____

Notes:

SUNDAY

Distance: _____

Time: _____

Speed: _____

Weather: _____

Calories burned: _____

Notes:

WEEKLY REVIEW

Total distance: _____

Total hours: _____

Average speed: _____

Total calories burned: _____

Weight: _____

Notes:

Week starting:_____

MONDAY

Distance: _____

Time: _____

Speed: _____

Weather: _____

Calories burned: _____

Notes:

TUESDAY

Distance: _____

Time: _____

Speed: _____

Weather: _____

Calories burned: _____

Notes:

WEDNESDAY

Distance: _____

Time: _____

Speed: _____

Weather: _____

Calories burned: _____

Notes:

THURSDAY

Distance: _____

Time: _____

Speed: _____

Weather: _____

Calories burned: _____

Notes:

FRIDAY

Distance:

Time:

Speed:

Weather:

Calories burned:

Notes:

SATURDAY

Distance:

Time:

Speed:

Weather:

Calories burned:

Notes:

SUNDAY

Distance:

Time:

Speed:

Weather:

Calories burned:

Notes:

WEEKLY REVIEW

Total distance:

Total hours:

Average speed:

Total calories burned:

Weight:

Notes:

Week starting:_____

MONDAY

Distance: _____

Time: _____

Speed: _____

Weather: _____

Calories burned: _____

Notes:

TUESDAY

Distance: _____

Time: _____

Speed: _____

Weather: _____

Calories burned: _____

Notes:

WEDNESDAY

Distance: _____

Time: _____

Speed: _____

Weather: _____

Calories burned: _____

Notes:

THURSDAY

Distance: _____

Time: _____

Speed: _____

Weather: _____

Calories burned: _____

Notes:

FRIDAY

Distance: _____

Time: _____

Speed: _____

Weather: _____

Calories burned: _____

Notes:

SATURDAY

Distance: _____

Time: _____

Speed: _____

Weather: _____

Calories burned: _____

Notes:

SUNDAY

Distance: _____

Time: _____

Speed: _____

Weather: _____

Calories burned: _____

Notes:

WEEKLY REVIEW

Total distance: _____

Total hours: _____

Average speed: _____

Total calories burned: _____

Weight: _____

Notes:

Week starting:_____

MONDAY

Distance:_____

Time:_____

Speed:_____

Weather:_____

Calories burned:_____

Notes:

TUESDAY

Distance:_____

Time:_____

Speed:_____

Weather:_____

Calories burned:_____

Notes:

WEDNESDAY

Distance:_____

Time:_____

Speed:_____

Weather:_____

Calories burned:_____

Notes:

THURSDAY

Distance:_____

Time:_____

Speed:_____

Weather:_____

Calories burned:_____

Notes:

FRIDAY

Distance: _____

Time: _____

Speed: _____

Weather: _____

Calories burned: _____

Notes:

SATURDAY

Distance: _____

Time: _____

Speed: _____

Weather: _____

Calories burned: _____

Notes:

SUNDAY

Distance: _____

Time: _____

Speed: _____

Weather: _____

Calories burned: _____

Notes:

WEEKLY REVIEW

Total distance: _____

Total hours: _____

Average speed: _____

Total calories burned: _____

Weight: _____

Notes:

Week starting:——————

MONDAY

Distance: ——————————

Time: ——————————

Speed: ——————————

Weather: ——————————

Calories burned: ——————————

Notes:

TUESDAY

Distance: ——————————

Time: ——————————

Speed: ——————————

Weather: ——————————

Calories burned: ——————————

Notes:

WEDNESDAY

Distance: ——————————

Time: ——————————

Speed: ——————————

Weather: ——————————

Calories burned: ——————————

Notes:

THURSDAY

Distance: ——————————

Time: ——————————

Speed: ——————————

Weather: ——————————

Calories burned: ——————————

Notes:

FRIDAY

Distance: _____

Time: _____

Speed: _____

Weather: _____

Calories burned: _____

Notes:

SATURDAY

Distance: _____

Time: _____

Speed: _____

Weather: _____

Calories burned: _____

Notes:

SUNDAY

Distance: _____

Time: _____

Speed: _____

Weather: _____

Calories burned: _____

Notes:

WEEKLY REVIEW

Total distance: _____

Total hours: _____

Average speed: _____

Total calories burned: _____

Weight: _____

Notes:

Week starting:_____

MONDAY

Distance:_____

Time:_____

Speed:_____

Weather:_____

Calories burned:_____

Notes:

TUESDAY

Distance:_____

Time:_____

Speed:_____

Weather:_____

Calories burned:_____

Notes:

WEDNESDAY

Distance:_____

Time:_____

Speed:_____

Weather:_____

Calories burned:_____

Notes:

THURSDAY

Distance:_____

Time:_____

Speed:_____

Weather:_____

Calories burned:_____

Notes:

FRIDAY

Distance: _____

Time: _____

Speed: _____

Weather: _____

Calories burned: _____

Notes:

SATURDAY

Distance: _____

Time: _____

Speed: _____

Weather: _____

Calories burned: _____

Notes:

SUNDAY

Distance: _____

Time: _____

Speed: _____

Weather: _____

Calories burned: _____

Notes:

WEEKLY REVIEW

Total distance: _____

Total hours: _____

Average speed: _____

Total calories burned: _____

Weight: _____

Notes:

Week starting:_____

MONDAY

Distance:_____

Time:_____

Speed:_____

Weather:_____

Calories burned:_____

Notes:

TUESDAY

Distance:_____

Time:_____

Speed:_____

Weather:_____

Calories burned:_____

Notes:

WEDNESDAY

Distance:_____

Time:_____

Speed:_____

Weather:_____

Calories burned:_____

Notes:

THURSDAY

Distance:_____

Time:_____

Speed:_____

Weather:_____

Calories burned:_____

Notes:

FRIDAY

Distance: _____

Time: _____

Speed: _____

Weather: _____

Calories burned: _____

Notes:

SATURDAY

Distance: _____

Time: _____

Speed: _____

Weather: _____

Calories burned: _____

Notes:

SUNDAY

Distance: _____

Time: _____

Speed: _____

Weather: _____

Calories burned: _____

Notes:

WEEKLY REVIEW

Total distance: _____

Total hours: _____

Average speed: _____

Total calories burned: _____

Weight: _____

Notes:

Week starting:_____

MONDAY

Distance:

Time:

Speed:

Weather:

Calories burned:

Notes:

TUESDAY

Distance:

Time:

Speed:

Weather:

Calories burned:

Notes:

WEDNESDAY

Distance:

Time:

Speed:

Weather:

Calories burned:

Notes:

THURSDAY

Distance:

Time:

Speed:

Weather:

Calories burned:

Notes:

FRIDAY

Distance:

Time:

Speed:

Weather:

Calories burned:

Notes:

SATURDAY

Distance:

Time:

Speed:

Weather:

Calories burned:

Notes:

SUNDAY

Distance:

Time:

Speed:

Weather:

Calories burned:

Notes:

WEEKLY REVIEW

Total distance:

Total hours:

Average speed:

Total calories burned:

Weight:

Notes:

Week starting:_____

MONDAY

Distance: _____

Time: _____

Speed: _____

Weather: _____

Calories burned: _____

Notes:

TUESDAY

Distance: _____

Time: _____

Speed: _____

Weather: _____

Calories burned: _____

Notes:

WEDNESDAY

Distance: _____

Time: _____

Speed: _____

Weather: _____

Calories burned: _____

Notes:

THURSDAY

Distance: _____

Time: _____

Speed: _____

Weather: _____

Calories burned: _____

Notes:

FRIDAY

Distance:

Time:

Speed:

Weather:

Calories burned:

Notes:

SATURDAY

Distance:

Time:

Speed:

Weather:

Calories burned:

Notes:

SUNDAY

Distance:

Time:

Speed:

Weather:

Calories burned:

Notes:

WEEKLY REVIEW

Total distance:

Total hours:

Average speed:

Total calories burned:

Weight:

Notes:

Week starting:_____

MONDAY

Distance:_____

Time:_____

Speed:_____

Weather:_____

Calories burned:_____

Notes:

TUESDAY

Distance:_____

Time:_____

Speed:_____

Weather:_____

Calories burned:_____

Notes:

WEDNESDAY

Distance:_____

Time:_____

Speed:_____

Weather:_____

Calories burned:_____

Notes:

THURSDAY

Distance:_____

Time:_____

Speed:_____

Weather:_____

Calories burned:_____

Notes:

FRIDAY

Distance: _____

Time: _____

Speed: _____

Weather: _____

Calories burned: _____

Notes:

SATURDAY

Distance: _____

Time: _____

Speed: _____

Weather: _____

Calories burned: _____

Notes:

SUNDAY

Distance: _____

Time: _____

Speed: _____

Weather: _____

Calories burned: _____

Notes:

WEEKLY REVIEW

Total distance: _____

Total hours: _____

Average speed: _____

Total calories burned: _____

Weight: _____

Notes:

Week starting:_____

MONDAY

Distance:_____

Time:_____

Speed:_____

Weather:_____

Calories burned:_____

Notes:

TUESDAY

Distance:_____

Time:_____

Speed:_____

Weather:_____

Calories burned:_____

Notes:

WEDNESDAY

Distance:_____

Time:_____

Speed:_____

Weather:_____

Calories burned:_____

Notes:

THURSDAY

Distance:_____

Time:_____

Speed:_____

Weather:_____

Calories burned:_____

Notes:

FRIDAY

Distance: _____

Time: _____

Speed: _____

Weather: _____

Calories burned: _____

Notes:

SATURDAY

Distance: _____

Time: _____

Speed: _____

Weather: _____

Calories burned: _____

Notes:

SUNDAY

Distance: _____

Time: _____

Speed: _____

Weather: _____

Calories burned: _____

Notes:

WEEKLY REVIEW

Total distance: _____

Total hours: _____

Average speed: _____

Total calories burned: _____

Weight: _____

Notes:

Week starting:_____

MONDAY

Distance:_____

Time:_____

Speed:_____

Weather:_____

Calories burned:_____

Notes:

TUESDAY

Distance:_____

Time:_____

Speed:_____

Weather:_____

Calories burned:_____

Notes:

WEDNESDAY

Distance:_____

Time:_____

Speed:_____

Weather:_____

Calories burned:_____

Notes:

THURSDAY

Distance:_____

Time:_____

Speed:_____

Weather:_____

Calories burned:_____

Notes:

FRIDAY

Distance: _____

Time: _____

Speed: _____

Weather: _____

Calories burned: _____

Notes:

SATURDAY

Distance: _____

Time: _____

Speed: _____

Weather: _____

Calories burned: _____

Notes:

SUNDAY

Distance: _____

Time: _____

Speed: _____

Weather: _____

Calories burned: _____

Notes:

WEEKLY REVIEW

Total distance: _____

Total hours: _____

Average speed: _____

Total calories burned: _____

Weight: _____

Notes:

Week starting:_____

MONDAY

Distance:_____

Time:_____

Speed:_____

Weather:_____

Calories burned:_____

Notes:

TUESDAY

Distance:_____

Time:_____

Speed:_____

Weather:_____

Calories burned:_____

Notes:

WEDNESDAY

Distance:_____

Time:_____

Speed:_____

Weather:_____

Calories burned:_____

Notes:

THURSDAY

Distance:_____

Time:_____

Speed:_____

Weather:_____

Calories burned:_____

Notes:

FRIDAY

Distance: _____

Time: _____

Speed: _____

Weather: _____

Calories burned: _____

Notes:

SATURDAY

Distance: _____

Time: _____

Speed: _____

Weather: _____

Calories burned: _____

Notes:

SUNDAY

Distance: _____

Time: _____

Speed: _____

Weather: _____

Calories burned: _____

Notes:

WEEKLY REVIEW

Total distance: _____

Total hours: _____

Average speed: _____

Total calories burned: _____

Weight: _____

Notes:

Week starting:_____

MONDAY

Distance:_____

Time:_____

Speed:_____

Weather:_____

Calories burned:_____

Notes:

TUESDAY

Distance:_____

Time:_____

Speed:_____

Weather:_____

Calories burned:_____

Notes:

WEDNESDAY

Distance:_____

Time:_____

Speed:_____

Weather:_____

Calories burned:_____

Notes:

THURSDAY

Distance:_____

Time:_____

Speed:_____

Weather:_____

Calories burned:_____

Notes:

FRIDAY

Distance: _____

Time: _____

Speed: _____

Weather: _____

Calories burned: _____

Notes:

SATURDAY

Distance: _____

Time: _____

Speed: _____

Weather: _____

Calories burned: _____

Notes:

SUNDAY

Distance: _____

Time: _____

Speed: _____

Weather: _____

Calories burned: _____

Notes:

WEEKLY REVIEW

Total distance: _____

Total hours: _____

Average speed: _____

Total calories burned: _____

Weight: _____

Notes:

Week starting:_____

MONDAY

Distance: _____

Time: _____

Speed: _____

Weather: _____

Calories burned: _____

Notes:

TUESDAY

Distance: _____

Time: _____

Speed: _____

Weather: _____

Calories burned: _____

Notes:

WEDNESDAY

Distance: _____

Time: _____

Speed: _____

Weather: _____

Calories burned: _____

Notes:

THURSDAY

Distance: _____

Time: _____

Speed: _____

Weather: _____

Calories burned: _____

Notes:

FRIDAY

Distance: _____

Time: _____

Speed: _____

Weather: _____

Calories burned: _____

Notes:

SATURDAY

Distance: _____

Time: _____

Speed: _____

Weather: _____

Calories burned: _____

Notes:

SUNDAY

Distance: _____

Time: _____

Speed: _____

Weather: _____

Calories burned: _____

Notes:

WEEKLY REVIEW

Total distance: _____

Total hours: _____

Average speed: _____

Total calories burned: _____

Weight: _____

Notes:

Notes

Notes

Notes

Notes

Notes

Printed in Great Britain
by Amazon